My First Pet

BUNNY

Douglas Bender

TABLE OF CONTENTS

A Pelican Book

SEAHORSE PUBLISHING

Teaching Tips for Caregivers and Teachers:

Research shows that one of the best ways for students to learn a new topic is to read about it.

Before Reading

- Read the title and predict what the book will be about.
- Read the "Words to Know" and discuss the meaning of each word.
- Read the back cover to see what the book is about.

During Reading

- When a student gets to a word that is unknown, ask them to look at the rest of the sentence to find clues to help with the meaning of the unknown word.
- Motivate students with praise and encouragement.

After Reading

- Discuss the main idea of the book.
- Ask students to give one detail that they learned in the book.

SIGHT WORDS

a	have	play
all	is	run
and	jump	some
big	like	this
black	long	to
brown	many	white
can	or	

WORDS TO KNOW

bunny

ears

fur

tails

whiskers

This is a **bunny**.

bunny

Bunnies can have black, white, or brown **fur**.

fur

Many bunnies have **tails**.

tails

Some bunnies have big **ears**.

ears

Some bunnies have long **whiskers**.

whiskers

All bunnies like to run, jump, and play!

INDEX

Written by: Douglas Bender
Design by: Under the Oaks Media
Series Development: James Earley
Editor: Kim Thompson

Photos: Shutterstock: Happy Monkey: cover; Cora Mueller: p. 5; Roselynne: p. 7; Oleksandr Lytvynenko: p. 9; Anna Ipatjeva: p. 11; vellot: p. 13; Rita Kochmarjova: p. 15

Library of Congress PCN Data
Bunny / Douglas Bender
My First Pet
ISBN 978-1-63897-433-8(hard cover)
ISBN 978-1-63897-548-9(paperback)
ISBN 978-1-63897-663-9(EPUB)
ISBN 978-1-63897-778-0(eBook)
Library of Congress Control Number: 2022932425

Printed in the United States of America.

Seahorse Publishing Company
www.seahorsepub.com

Published in the United States
Seahorse Publishing
PO Box 771325
Coral Springs, FL 33077

SEAHORSE PUBLISHING